WHAT HAD HAPPENED WAS...

A realistic way to view a deal of a lifetime.

Chaeeda,
Its always great
to see you. Thank you
for your support. We go way
back + now its time to
build some WEALTH together.

Clyde

Clyde Anderson

PARAMIND PUBLICATIONS
A *Shift* in Thinking

ParaMind Publications

Copyright ©2005, 2012 by Clyde Anderson

Published by ParaMind Publications, LLC
2090 Baker Road, Ste. 304-171, Kennesaw, Georgia 30144

Library of Congress Control Number: 2004098467

ISBN 978-0-9762738-8-2

Printed in the United States of America

www.paramindpublications.com

SECOND EDITION

Dedicated to all who have inspired me through their trials and triumphs and have uttered the words "What Had Happened Was," I truly thank you. It is because of your stories and courage I'm able to open my heart, listen and understand how to help others. God bless everyone who reads this book. May the understanding you develop, help sharpen your sword.

Proverb 27:17 *Iron sharpens iron, so one man sharpens another*
(NEW INTERNATIONAL VERSION)

To all my friends

Character | ˈkarɪktər | n. a person's good reputation.

Contents

Introduction

Welcome to Reality

S omewhere between perfect bliss and rock bottom is a town called Reality. Life in Reality is a fast paced rat race; similar to the world we live in. Its filled with everyday, ordinary residents just trying to make it. People either survive, or get left behind.

Reality can be harsh to those unprepared for challenges, or generous to those who understand how the game is played. One thing that separate these two classes of people in Reality, is good character. Its also the one asset every resident needs to take advantage of the Special Deal.

Is your character good enough to
handle something special?
Welcome to Reality.

Chapter One

The Special Deal Is Coming...

*"Whatever affects one directly, affects all
indirectly. I can never be what I ought to be
until you are what you ought to be. This
is the interrelated structure of reality."*
~MARTIN LUTHER KING, JR.

The dawn of a new day brought exciting news to Reality. As the good citizens wiped sleep from their eyes and prepared for another day of hustle and bustle in the city, Reality was transformed with signs that welcomed the most amazing surprise. Green billboards with hypnotic gold letters read:

**Get Ready
The Special Deal
Is Coming!
It's the deal of a lifetime
What you've been waiting for,
the answer to all
your questions; Freedom,
the ability to live out your
dreams!**

It had been a long time since anything this good had happened in Reality. News of the Special Deal spread quickly. It was advertised on all the major television and radio stations, and popped up constantly on the internet. The entire town buzzed with curiosity, wondering what The Special Deal was all about.

One of the first residents to notice the Special Deal was Tugood Tubetru. He had seen a sign posted on a tree while fetching the Daily Economic Journal from his driveway.

"Well, what is this all about," Tugood Tubetru thought as he read the bright green sign with shimmering gold letters. "Hum, I may be interested in the Special Deal."

Tugood grabbed the paper then headed towards the kitchen to finish his morning cup of coffee before he drove to work. As he glanced over the headlines, there was a feature article about the Special Deal. Tugood read every word carefully, including a small disclaimer summarizing certain requirements to take advantage of the Special Deal.

"Lets see now, it says to possess a strong Character Profile, good reputation and have a Financial Success Plan," Tugood Tubetru said processing the information. "Why that's easy for me. I'm going to start right away. This is the best opportunity yet!"

One of the requirements was to possess a strong Character Profile. Tugood knew he had an excellent reputation, therefore the first requirement was nothing to worry about. Tugood also knew he could verify his good reputation with a copy of his Character Report. It's important to review your Character Report at least twice a year. If there are any concerns, problems or mistakes, they can be solved by addressing them early.

Tugood Tubetru was so excited about the Special Deal, he decided to be proactive and contact the Special Deal Headquarters. The Special Deal Headquarters was a particular facility where Character Profile information and character history data was processed and stored. They also governed all decisions regarding the Special Deal.

Tugood dialed the phone number provided in the article and patiently waited for someone to answer his call. A few moments later a representative with a warm and pleasant voice answered.

"Good Morning Special Deal Headquarters, how can I direct your call?"

"Yes, good morning," Tugood Tubetru replied. "I would like to inquire about the Special Deal?"

"Great! First let me have your name and personal identification number so I can access your Character Report. From there I will analyze your report to determine your specific requirements," the representative continued.

"That sounds like a good plan!" Tugood Tubetru exclaimed.

Tugood cheerfully gave the representative his name and personal identification number, which also unveiled his personal character history. The representative put Tugood Tubetru on hold while his information was being processed. After a brief pause, the representative returned.

"Tugood Tubetru your Character Report looks flawless. Your report shows a history of honoring your commitments and maintaining a Financial Success Plan, therefore you are pre-approved for the Special Deal. Your only requirements to receive the Special Deal are to enhance your Financial Success Plan and keep your character report and reputation in good standing."

"Thank you so much, this is so wonderful," Tugood Tubetru replied.

He thanked the representative for her time and ended the call. With a few minutes to spare before driving to work, Tugood quickly turned on the radio to get the latest weather and traffic update and heard the radio personality talking about the Special Deal. He said some good residents in Reality would not qualify for the Special Deal because of poor character decisions. Many had taken on more than they could handle and their character was in jeopardy of being tarnished. But that was not the case with Tugood Tubetru. You see in Reality, Tugood Tubetru was considered special because his personal situation was not like the other residents. He was considered the one to call whenever good character was required.

Tugood remembered being taught as a teenager that building good character is a valuable commodity that determines self worth. He learned important lessons of responsibility that influenced his ability to make good decisions. Tugood applied life skills imparted by his parents to create a solid Financial Success Plan which kept him on track to honor his commitments. He has remained faithful to his parents' advice and continues to sustain a positive character future.

Our character is basically a composite of our habits. Because they are consistent, often unconscious patterns, they constantly, daily, express our character.
~STEPHEN COVEY

If you build good habits you increase the odds of building great character

Chapter Two

If You Say You Don't, Then You Won't

*"You cannot escape the responsibility
of tomorrow by evading it today."*
~ABRAHAM LINCOLN

Couden Careless sat on the sofa feeling sorry for himself. He had just lost another minimum wage job. Without steady employment he could not escape his growing pile of debt.

"This is impossible. How am I supposed to make any real money when I can't even keep a job," Couden said hopelessly. "I've got collection companies calling me everyday about this bill and that bill...oh I give up!"

Couden was frustrated with his circumstances. He couldn't figure out how to change his life or his debt situation. Couden thought about filing bankruptcy when he remembered the Special Deal.

"Who needs a job anyway when you can have freedom," Couden thought. "All my problems will be solved when I get my hands on that Special Deal."

Couden searched his modest apartment for a pen and paper to write down all the things he would change about his life when he noticed a green envelope with golden letters from the Special Deal Headquarters.

"How did I miss this?" he wondered. "Oh well. It must have been here for a couple of days since I haven't checked the mail in a while."

When you have as many collection letters as Couden Careless, it's easy to avoid the mail. He gazed at the envelope and slid his fingers across the gold embossing before ripping it open. Couden pulled out a card that read:

**Get Ready
The Special Deal
Is Coming!
It's the deal of a lifetime
What you've been waiting for,
the answer to all
your questions; Freedom,
the ability to live out your
dreams!**

"This is just what I was waiting for... a chance of a lifetime!" Couden shouted.

Although Couden was very excited about the Special Deal, he didn't consider the minimum standards set by the Special Deal Headquarters. But when a character report looks as horrible as his, you have to wonder why Couden Careless thought he would qualify in the first place.

You see in Reality, Couden Careless was never educated about having good character. He was never taught how certain decisions could negatively affect his character report. Unknowingly, he started his own downward spiral. Tragically, he was a victim waiting to happen when he received his first character card. With that character card, came another and another. Couden thought it was great!

He used a fresh reputation and bought things when he didn't have the money...genius! Then the bills started pouring in and it was hard to juggle all the payments, especially when Couden was in between jobs. He got so deep into debt that he simply let his situation go. Couden didn't care anymore and his new reputation quickly tarnished. He stopped paying his bills, bounced checks and created collections trailing miles behind. As a result of his negligent actions, his character suffered horribly and caused his report to appear derogatory to anyone who viewed it, including employers. Since Couden never viewed a copy of his character profile, he was clueless to the information being reported.

After reading the Special Deal card, Couden opened a letter that gave him a rude awakening:

Special Deal Headquarters

Couden Careless
N. Limbo Lane
Reality, USA 24683

Mr. Careless,

Upon careful review of your character report we regret
to inform that you are ineligible to qualify at this
time for the Special Deal. Your pre-approval status is
based on meeting certain qualifications that determine
your ability to handle something special. Your report
shows consistent lack of responsibility and derogatory
accounts with creditors, which has negatively affected
your reputation and your character report. Our records
indicate you've made numerous personal and financial
mistakes stemming from bad decisions and have done
little to satisfy your obligations.

If you would like to be considered for the Special Deal,
the Special Deal Headquarters is willing to extend a
Second Chance offer under a probationary period. To
qualify for the Second Chance Deal you must fulfill the
following requirements:

1. Maintain a job for at least six months.
2. Create a Financial Success Plan.
3. Write a letter explaining what had happened and
    what you have learned from your past mistakes.

These are your requirements. After you have completed
these things, your information will then be processed
for consideration.

Sincerely,
Special Deal Headquarters

"Whatever," Couden said sarcastically finishing the letter. "I know my reputation can't be that bad, can it? Besides I heard about somebody getting the Special Deal with worse character than mine, so I know I should get it."

In Reality, this was only a myth. Receiving the Special Deal would be a huge opportunity for Couden Careless. One that could possibly pay off old debt and help him start over pending a solid plan to achieve financial success. He could not afford to mess this up. If only Couden thought about it that way. Unfortunately, some residents of Reality have a lot to learn. Couden Careless was one of them.

Life is a series of experiences, each one of which makes us bigger, even though sometimes it is hard to realize this. For the world was built to develop character, and we must learn that the setbacks and grieves which we endure help us in our marching onward.

~HENRY FORD

We must recognize that our setbacks can serve as opportunities that inspire us to greatness

Chapter Three

Mr. Me Too

*Man wants to live, but it is useless to hope
that this desire will dictate all his actions.*
~ALBERT CAMUS

The buzz surrounding the Special Deal continued to build, yet one resident in particular did not have time to notice all the excitement. It was Reality's most flamboyant, Dee Joneses. Dee had been quite busy overseeing major renovations to her property. She had seen some of her neighbors make similar changes to their homes and could not be outdone. She was determined to have the best looking home in the neighborhood no matter the cost. Besides, her character card could handle it; so she thought. The appearance of wealth was very important to Dee. Sometimes she went to the extreme just to have the right look.

One sunny afternoon, Dee was standing in the middle of her backyard admiring her latest creation. A customized, voice-activated, fresh water spa tub installed on her covered temperature controlled patio, courtesy of reputation and character. In awe of her all weather retreat, Dee overheard a familiar voice.

"That sounds like my next door neighbor," Dee thought. "What is Virginia talking about now?"

Dee had never cared for Virginia's "irritating" voice, but today Virginia seemed to be bragging about something that intrigued her very much. Dee continued to listen closely as she heard her neighbor say:

**Get Ready
The Special Deal
Is Coming!
It's the deal of a lifetime
What you've been waiting for,
the answer to all
your questions; Freedom,
the ability to live out your
dreams!**

"What is this Special Deal and why does Virginia know so much…in fact, too much information about it!" Dee screamed. "I have to act fast so I can have the deal of a lifetime before Virginia or anyone else in Reality."

Determined to find the Special Deal, Dee rushed into the kitchen, grabbed the keys to her new luxury car and ran out the front door. Before she could open the car door, she heard Virginia calling.

"Hey Dee…how are you doing today?" Virginia asked snidely.

"Great, just great Virginia. What do you want?"

"Oh nothing, well it is something but…did you receive a letter in the mail about the Special Deal?" "I did."

"Of course Virginia, you know I always keep up with the latest."

Dee was furious at Virginia for asking about the Special Deal especially since she didn't know about it. She pretended to be in the loop hiding her true feelings from Virginia. Now Dee was on a serious mission to get the Special Deal and Virginia was wasting her time. In the middle of their conversation, Dee abruptly hopped in her car, slammed the door and sped off leaving Virginia stunned and puzzled, wondering what just happened.

Dee raced through the neighborhood reaching for her cell phone in the passenger seat. She wanted to call information and obtain the location of the Special Deal.

"I'll get to the bottom of this," driving madly. "It's obvious they don't know who I am!" she declared.

Grabbing her phone, Dee noticed a small stack of envelopes on the floor of her car. She recalled taking the mail out of her briefcase and placing it under the seat as she drove to work yesterday. Blast! She had forgotten about it and left it in the car. When Dee stopped at a traffic light, she decided to check the mail for any new character card offers. She loved getting character cards. It was like having a clean reputation every time she went shopping. Then out of the pile of offers emerged a green envelope with golden letters from the Special Deal Headquarters.

Oblivious to the green light and the flow of traffic, Dee gazed at the envelope. The shiny gold letters were hypnotizing. Eager to read its contents, she ripped open the envelope. Dee quickly skimmed through the letter but paused when she read the shocking news:

Special Deal Headquarters

Dee Joneses
2 Keep Up Way
Reality, USA 24680

Ms. Joneses,

Upon careful review of your character report we regret to inform that you are ineligible to qualify at this time for the Special Deal. Your pre-approval status is based on meeting certain qualifications that determine your ability to handle something special. Your report shows consistent overindulgence and abuse from maxing out accounts with creditors, which has tarnished your reputation and negatively affected your character report. Our records indicate that you've made numerous personal and financial mistakes stemming from your need to keep up with trends and buy items you really don't need or can barely afford.

If you would like to be considered for the Special Deal, the Special Deal Headquarters is willing to extend a Second Chance offer under a probationary period. To qualify for the Second Chance Deal you must fulfill the following requirements:

1. Only buy items you need instead of items you want.
2. Begin to pay off as much debt as possible.
3. Develop a Financial Success Plan.

These are your requirements. After you have completed these things, your information will then be processed for consideration.

Sincerely,
Special Deal Headquarters

"This can't be right," Dee said disconcertedly. "Besides, if my reputation is so bad, why do I keep getting character card offers in the mail?"

You see in Reality, Dee Joneses didn't realize she had a serious problem. She loved material things and using character cards to buy them! Dee adored being the talk of the town because of her possessions. This gave her power and fed her greed for more. With one of the most beautiful homes in the neighborhood, a new top of the line luxury car, a great corporate job she was lucky to have with good income as well as full benefits, how could you ignore Dee Joneses?

Dee thought her life was great; so did everyone else in Reality. Except there was just one problem...Dee was going broke. She did not take her lifestyle seriously. Had Dee thought about her situation, she would have realized that she spent the majority of what she earns on her wonderful lifestyle. When her sizable monthly income was gone, she used character cards to take up the slack. As a result of her lavish existence and constant greed, her reputation went from positive to marginal, drastically affecting her character.

The debt that Dee had accumulated, exceeded her monthly income and caused problems each month. She sometimes had difficulty paying all of her bills by the due date. Unfortunately, that was the price Dee Joneses paid for living the high life.

Cars blew there horns for Dee to move while she sat stunned in her car. The idea of having to complete certain requirements to qualify was embarrassing. After all, maxing out her character cards was her decision and no one else's. She believed she was entitled to the Special Deal, and no one should have the right to question her worthiness.

After gaining her composure and going with the flow of traffic, Dee considered her requirements for the Second Chance Deal and decided to follow through.

"I don't care what type of deal I get as long as I get the chance to have freedom and live out my dreams. Virginia and all the rest of Reality will never know the difference anyway," Dee thought. "Even if I have to change my lifestyle for a few months, it won't be the first time I've done something drastic to be on top...and it won't be the last either."

Charged with a new mission Dee Joneses steered her car towards home to begin work on her requirements. Along the way, she daydreamed about all the wonderful things she would buy when she got the Special Deal. Some things will never change.

Be more concerned with your character than your reputation, because your character is what you really are, while your reputation is merely what others think you are.
~JOHN WOODEN

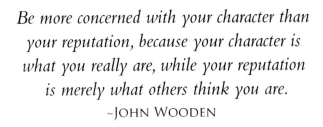

It's not about what you have but rather who you are, the type of person you are when no one else sees you

Chapter Four

You Get Out What You Put In

*It is a wretched waste to be gratified with
mediocrity when the excellent lies before us.*
~ISAAC DISRAELI

Jestu Getby had completed his fourth personal call
at work when he decided not to answer any more
incoming calls. He preferred daydreaming about the
perfect life, full of success and happiness. All he needed to
do was figure out how to quit his dead end job. He often
did this after answering about twenty customer service
calls, the minimum required to fulfill his daily quota.

You see in Reality, Jestu Getby never saw a need to
do more than what's required when performing a task.
He firmly believed in doing just enough to get by. He
often complained about his job but in a sense, he enjoyed

it. His job nurtured the mentality of performing minimal duties with just enough pay to survive. Jestu had perks too. He took extra long lunches and got other coworkers to clock out for him when he wanted to go home early. This was his way of life. Do just enough to get by and everything would be all right.

A fifth personal call was in motion when an instant message popped up on the computer screen. It read:

**Get Ready
The Special Deal
Is Coming!
It's the deal of a lifetime
What you've been waiting for,
the answer to all
your questions; Freedom,
the ability to live out your
dreams!**

"What in the world," Jestu murmured looking over both shoulders to see if there were any suspicious looking coworkers making jokes.

Writing the message off as an office hoax, Jestu remembered the Special Deal from the radio a few weeks ago. He rolled the cursor over the message then a letter appeared in the middle of the screen. It stated:

Special Deal Headquarters

Gestu Getby
22 Minimal Drive
Reality, USA 24682

Mr. Getby,

Upon careful review of your character report we regret
to inform that you are ineligible to qualify at this time
for the Special Deal. Your pre-approval status is based
on meeting certain qualifications that determine your
ability to handle something special. Your report shows
a slothful reputation and insignificant character, along
with marginal accounts with creditors, which has
negatively affected your character report. Our records
indicate you've made numerous personal and financial
mistakes stemming from your lack of effort to do more
yet still expecting to have a better life someday.

If you would like to be considered for the Special Deal,
the Special Deal Headquarters is willing to extend a
Second Chance offer under a probationary period. To
qualify for the Second Chance Deal you must fulfill the
following requirements:

1. Set some life goals.
2. Develop a Financial Success Plan.

These are your requirements. After you have completed
these things, your information will then be processed
for consideration.

Sincerely,
Special Deal Headquarters

"So this is the deal everyone is crazy about," Jestu said after reading the letter. "I don't understand why anyone would go crazy over doing extra work just to get a deal... that's not special."

Jestu Getby could not accept why anyone would work for something now and wait to have it later. His logic led him to believe that some residents in Reality receive things that appear to be special all the time by doing the same amount of work, or even less. He couldn't possibly fathom the thought of doing anything extra to get something special in return.

Jestu read the letter again and said, "I don't see how completing these requirements will benefit me anyway. My reputation isn't the best, but it's gotten me this far... right?" "I can live with that."

Jestu did not understand that following through with his requirements was an opportunity to help his slothful reputation and improve his history of being lazy.

You see in Reality, Jestu Getby had a problem breaking old habits of making bad decisions that affect character. He was never taught how certain decisions and actions could have a negative affect on his character report and tarnish his reputation. So naturally he did not realize that procrastinating, paying bills late and missing payment arrangements would cause his character and reputation to become second class.

Jestu's lack of responsibility caused him to live moment-to-moment and unprepared for the future. If events outside the norm happened, which they did often, or he missed just one paycheck, Jestu would have difficulty living at his current modest level.

Jestu thought about his life and wondered if he had what it took to get the Special Deal. He deliberated for hours it seemed, but finally came to a decision.

"Okay, I'll go for it," Jestu said confidently. "The requirements don't seem that bad, but the second I feel like I'm doing more work than I have to, I'll quit." "Maybe I'll get lucky and change my boring life."

Character isn't something you were born with and can't change, like your fingerprints. It's something you weren't born with and must take responsibility for forming.
~JIM ROHN

❦

You must choose if doing the minimum will afford you the results you seek in life

The Special Deal Is Almost Here!

How Will You Handle Commitment

Chapter Five

Adversity in the Midst of Opportunity

*A total commitment is paramount to
reaching the ultimate in performance.*
~TOM FLORES

O ver six months had passed and just about every resident
in Reality knew about the Special Deal. Some of the
residents were already busy fulfilling their Special Deal
requirements while others procrastinated, including
Couden Careless. Still unemployed and feeling sorry for
himself, Couden was relaxing at a friend's house when
he saw a commercial on the television screen.

> Have you fulfilled your Special
> Deal requirements?
> Time is running out!
> Don't miss the chance to
> live out your dreams!

"Oh, no! I forgot about the Special Deal," Couden said jumping off the sofa.

He immediately thought about his offer letter. He had opened the letter some months ago and had no idea of where it could be. Without steady employment, Couden had to move in with a friend since he could not afford rent on his own. There was a chance the letter could have been thrown away during the move by mistake. Possibly loosing the only opportunity he had to change his life, Couden scrambled to find his offer letter. He searched everywhere he believed it could be. As he rummaged through one of his old gym bags, he found something balled up with old juice stains on it.

"I hope this isn't it, looking like this," Couden said nervously.

Unsure of what he discovered, Couden carefully opened the balled paper and saw it was his offer letter after all.

"I don't know how this ended up in my bag," he thought. "I haven't used this bag in months." Couden Careless read the letter over to refresh his memory.

He thought about all the time he had wasted doing nothing when he could have been working on his requirements. But Couden always shrugged off his responsibilities. Now he had to work double time if it wasn't too late.

Convinced he had nothing left to lose Couden decided to work on his requirements. First he had to secure a job, then create a Financial Success Plan then finally write a letter explaining why his character and reputation were so bad. Since he didn't have a job, or even know what a Financial Success Plan was about, Couden decided to work on his explanation letter. After creating several drafts he decided his efforts were good enough and settled on a final letter. It read:

To Whom It May Concern:

I'm writing this letter because I was told I have a bad reputation and need to explain what had happened so I can receive the Special Deal.

First, none of this is my fault. My parents never taught me how to make good decisions. I am a helpless victim of Reality. Of course I have made some bad choices but it all started when I was younger so I don't think I should be held responsible. I was just a kid.

Second, the character card companies should be the ones to explain. They gave me cards all the time knowing my reputation wasn't the best and I didn't have a job most of the time. I did what any normal resident would have done. I took the offers and used them to live on. I know I didn't pay the bills on time but how could I? I didn't have steady income or a reliable car so how am I supposed to pay my bills or mail my bills?

Finally, I think that it is only fair for you to reconsider. I deserve the Special Deal for all the hardships I've been through. The only way for a person like me to start over is with the Special Deal.

Yours truly,
Couden Careless

"My letter will surely convince the Special Deal Headquarters," Couden thought. "This kind of thing happens all the time."

Couden Careless felt a sense of accomplishment. He was proud of himself for creating what he considered to be a sensible letter. Just as Couden was about to submit his explanation letter he noticed there was a deadline and it had expired!

"How could I have missed this?" Couden moaned. "I was never told I had a deadline!"

Frustrated and confused he tossed his letter in the air. Couden was heated and needed to take his frustrations out on someone so he called the Special Deal Headquarters to give them a piece of his mind. He felt as though the Special Deal Headquarters had set him up to fail.

Couden grabbed the phone. He dialed the number and waited impatiently for someone to answer his call. Listening to the phone ring, he started thinking about his life before the Special Deal.

"My life was okay by my standards until this deal had me jumping through hoops," he mumbled under his breath.

In Reality, Couden's life was nothing to be desired. Finally the customer service representative answered the call and Couden gave her an ear full of excuses.

"I have been misled about this Special Deal. I thought I had all the time I wanted to fulfill my requirements," he screamed. "I was about to submit my explanation letter when I noticed a deadline in small print. Because the date was too small for me to read, its too late to submit my explanation letter and claim my Special Deal."

"What are you going to do about it?" he demanded.

The silence on the other end was unnerving. Couden continued to rant on and on about how he didn't understand why his past mattered so much anyway. As he further justified his mistakes, the customer service representative asked him to hold. The representative transferred his call to the Second Chance department so he could vent with them. After holding for 10 solid minutes, Couden heard another voice on the other end of the phone. However, this representative had an attitude just like his but she was not in the mood for excuses.

"Please be quiet and listen to what I have to say. I've heard your situation before and I am not moved. I've spoken to hundreds of people alone today and they all had some sort of excuse of why they missed the deadline, or why they had certain reputation issues that prevented them from getting the deal," she continued.

It was hard for the representative to listen to the same stories over and over especially without evidence to back them up.

"You should have been more responsible with your reputation in the past, if you expect to get a Special Deal in the future. Only people who have taken the time to establish and maintain a good character report will enjoy the pleasure of getting the Special Deal. A bad reputation will harm your character report and the terms of how you receive future opportunities will be a lot harder."

A blank stare appeared across Couden's face as the representative concluded her lecture.

"You could have avoided several of the pitfalls you fell into. If you were only educated on what it means to establish a good reputation and how it affects your character profile, maybe your situation would have been a lot different."

Couden was ready to implode! "How dare she tell me I am uneducated?"

Couden wanted to let the representative have it when she said something to calm his fury. She told him he could still qualify for the deal under a special "Change Your Life or Else" clause.

You see in Reality, the representative started to feel bad that Couden Careless never learned how to establish a good reputation. She couldn't go back in time to help him avoid his mistakes, but she could help him find solutions to his errors and possibly start over. The problem was, she had seen so many like him repeat the same mistakes over and over. This caused her to question every story she heard, yet sometimes she managed to give certain callers another chance to prove themselves.

The representative explained the conditions of his new offer. The final requirements were to attend a character education class, complete his Financial Success Plan and secure steady employment wherever he could find it. When the requirements were completed, the Special Deal could possibly be his. Couden Careless concluded his conversation with the representative and applauded himself for handling the situation sternly.

"Yeah well I guess I told her huh…and I still get the chance to live out my dreams," Couden thought. "Oh wait a minute! I don't know where to go for my class."

Without details regarding the class, Couden decided he had time to wait.

The life of an uneducated man is as useless as the tail of a dog which neither covers its rear end, nor protects it from the bites of insects.
~CHANAKYA

You must remember that ignorance is not bliss

Ignorance: Lack of knowledge

Chapter Six

Needs Vs. Wants

*Dreams do come true, if we only wish hard
enough. You can have anything in life if
you will sacrifice everything else for it.*
~JAMES M. BARRIE

Across town sitting in the far corner of her bedroom, shaking, sweating and tightly gripping her character card was Dee Joneses. It had been over six months since she had used a character card. She hadn't made any new purchases except for food, gas and bare necessities. Committing to her requirements to get the Special Deal was driving Dee crazy. She cringed every time she noticed her neighbors with new household items and trendy new clothes. She felt as though her material possessions were old and tattered even though she had bought some of those treasures only six months ago.

You see in Reality, Dee was a victim of the "Christmas Scenario." Remember how you wanted certain toys for Christmas so badly that you thought about them every month? The big day finally arrives and you receive your gifts but it was a matter of time before that new feeling wore off. This was how Dee felt about everything she bought. She never understood the idea of delayed gratification.

Although Dee was a consumerholic, she had put forth a tremendous effort to stop frivolous spending. So much so, she couldn't concentrate on paying off her debt as required by the Special Deal Headquarters. Besides, Dee believed that since she wasn't spending, there wasn't any debt to repay. She forgot about her accumulated debt. As far as Dee was concerned, that was in the past. She also forgot about her Financial Success Plan. The only thing that kept her going was the Special Deal. Soon it could be hers and her life would be changed forever. So creating a Financial Success Plan was unnecessary when you could have freedom.

All of Dee's sweating and trembling was going to pay off if she could honor her commitments. But it was hard for her to stay focused on completing her requirements. Sometimes Dee would get so delirious from spending withdrawals that she would make price tags to put on her old cloths so she could pretend they were new and buy them all over again. No matter how delirious she would get, nothing was going to prevent her from getting the Special Deal, especially since her rival, Virginia, had found out about it first. Just as Dee was renewing her faith towards honoring her commitments, she turned on the television and saw the Network Spending Channel. There was an exclusive collection available for five minutes to its preferred platinum customers only.

"I'm a preferred platinum customer! This collection is perfect for me," Dee exclaimed. For a brief moment Dee forgot her requirements. "But I can't take advantage of it this time. If I do, I will lose my Special Deal and risk the chance to live out my dreams."

Dee was disappointed. She could not buy anything from the collection or else loose the deal. But after viewing the collection for a few minutes, she recognized it was the same one she had seen Virginia wearing the previous day.

"I can't let Virginia or anyone else out do me!" Dee shouted.

Something deep inside told Dee she had to have this offer. Suddenly she let out a horrible, loud grunt. Sometimes Dee didn't understand why she did the things she did.

You see in Reality, Dee believed that whenever she wanted something it should be hers to have. Maybe it was something that stemmed from her childhood. Maybe Dee's parents couldn't afford to buy nice things, or perhaps it was the opposite. Maybe her parents bought everything she wanted as a child and as an adult, the cycle continues. Who knows, but Dee was stuck between having the Special Deal and the platinum collection. She had to make a decision. All the sudden, Dee had the brilliant idea to take advantage of the platinum collection in secret.

"The Special Deal Headquarters already examined my character report before they sent the Second Chance letter, therefore no one would have to know about the purchase until after the Special Deal arrived," Dee thought. "What a plan. I hope it works!"

Dee cheerfully grabbed her cell phone to call the Network Spending Channel. She felt really good about scheming the Special Deal Headquarters, then her phone rang. She answered the call but it was only a recording. Ironically, the recording was from the Special Deal Headquarters. It was a courtesy call to make sure she was honoring her commitments to receive the Special Deal. Dee could not believe what had happened. This must have been divine intervention.

Dee felt foolish for risking the Special Deal. She couldn't believe she was willing to give up freedom for a few minutes of temporary pleasure. Delayed gratification was hard. With that thought, Dee hung up the phone and decided to play her department store game again.

"Back to putting tags on my old clothes. Something has to take my mind off of waiting for my Special Deal to arrive."

The gratification of wealth is not found in mere possession or in lavish expenditure, but in its wise application.
~MIGUEL DE CERVANTES

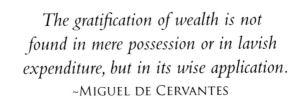

If we let our wants dictate our attitude, we'll be going in perpetual circles

Chapter Seven

Making Easy Things Difficult

*Faith has to do with things that are not seen
and hope with things that are not at hand.*
~THOMAS AQUINAS

Jestu Getby was ready to give up on the Special Deal. The previous months had been very rough for him. Committing to his requirements had Jestu going in circles. First, he was supposed to create a Financial Success Plan, which he knew nothing about. He made payment arrangements to bring his accounts current but without organization, he missed important dates to keep his arrangements.

His second requirement was to set some life goals, which Jestu struggled to complete as well. How was he supposed to set life goals if he was busy working and paying bills? Jestu lived a mediocre lifestyle although he dreamed of doing more with his life. His dead end job barely provided enough money to live on, so enjoying life and having fun was not realistic. It was hard for Jestu to develop a success plan and set life goals in the midst of a lifestyle he didn't want. Furthermore, he didn't know what type of goals and plans to develop anyway. How was Jestu supposed to plan for success, when it just seemed to happen if you're lucky, or so he thought?

Jestu claimed he wanted to change his life and do something different. But he had already convinced himself that the system was not set up for him to succeed. Jestu believed his job already required so much of him that it was hard to do anything else. He wasn't willing to work outside the job to have the kind of lifestyle he constantly daydreamed about.

"This is just too much for me to handle. Maybe the Special Deal is out of my league after all," he said. "I'm too tired to think. All I want to do is go back to the way things were before the Special Deal."

Life was easier and simpler for Jestu when all he had to do was follow his trusty daily routine. It went like this…get up, go to work, eat, sleep…get up, go to work, eat, sleep…and hope to catch a couple of hours of Reality television. Sound exciting?

Getting the Special Deal would be wonderful for Jestu but without determination or the ability to handle commitments, he would have to pass. What a shame to let a little extra work stand in the way of freedom.

All greatness of character is dependent on individuality. The man who has no other existence than that which he partakes in common with all around him, will never have any other than an existence of mediocrity.
~JAMES F. COOPER

We must realize our only opponent is in the mirror

Chapter Eight

Discipline Pays Well

*Hard work has made it easy. That is
my secret. That is why I win.*
~NADIA COMANECI

The following morning, Tugood Tubetru was looking
over his Financial Success Plan while sorting through
his daily mail. He had to be cautious of what he opened
and discarded these days. He had discovered an erroneous
charge account on his character report several months
ago. Fortunately for Tugood, he kept good records and
was able to successfully remove the error. Keeping his
character report clear of bogus accusations was very
important to maintain a good report.

As he organized the stack of letters, he saw a green
envelope with gold embossing from the Special Deal

Headquarters. Tugood eagerly opened the envelope and read the letter inside:

Special Deal Headquarters

Tugood Tubetru
1 Perfect Circle
Reality, USA 24681

Tugood Tubetru,

Congratulations! The Special Deal Headquarters is proud to present you with the Special Deal. Your hard work, dedication and commitment to preserving good character is applauded. Your ability to make good decisions and maintain a success plan, has allowed you to overcome character and financial obstacles where others have failed.

We, at the Special Deal Headquarters, view you as a role model for the character challenged. We thank you for being a responsible resident and taking ownership for your character actions. According to our updated records, you have handled your requirements as agreed. As a result your character rating can open doors that money can't buy.

Expect to receive your Special Deal within 24 hours. When your Special Deal arrives, please enjoy. Use it responsibly, which we know you will.

Sincerely,
Special Deal Chairperson

Tugood Tubetru was ecstatic!

"I can't believe this is happening. I am so grateful for this opportunity and will use it wisely to carry out my life's mission," Tugood vowed.

All of Tugood's hard work paid off, and it definitely takes wise choices to maintain a good character profile. It takes constant vigilance. Like anything worth achieving, the more you do it, the easier it becomes. This time Tugood Tubetru was rewarded with the Special Deal... freedom, the ability to live out his dreams.

But you see in Reality, Tugood was already receiving the rewards of a good character profile. He received great rates on his home and car loans as well as other financial perks. He was trustworthy and dependable so his creditors always took chances when he needed to borrow on his character. Tugood made sacrifices, delayed gratification, listened to what others told him about making the right decisions and lived within his Financial Success plan.

Getting the Special Deal was the pinnacle, especially since Tugood hadn't expected to get the deal so soon. Thanks to his diligence and desire to have more out of life, he would soon experience the freedom to live out his dreams.

In Reality, being responsible is what separates the winners from the losers and sometimes the winners can seem too good to be true.

Discipline is based on pride, on meticulous attention to details, and on mutual respect and confidence. Discipline must be a habit so ingrained that it is stronger than the excitement of the goal or the fear of failure.
~GARY RYAN BLAIR

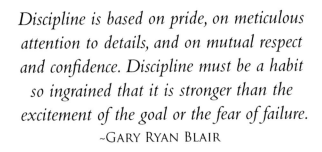

We must remember what we want and be willing to sacrifice to get it

The Time Has Come

How Will You Handle Your Fate

Chapter Nine

Move or Get Run Over

*Great achievement is usually born of great
sacrifice, and is never the result of selfishness.*
~NAPOLEON HILL

It had been almost a year since the Special Deal made
its debut in Reality. You could still see the bright green
signs with big gold letters posted around town. Everyone
was still buzzing with excitement. Others were holding
their breath until they learned their fate with the Special
Deal. Everyone that is, but Couden Careless.

It was a really stressful time for him. Thankfully he
had secured a new job and started his Financial Success
Plan, but the character class he was supposed to take
started today. It seemed like Couden Careless finally
decided to change his ways and get his act together
for the sake of the deal. Without the Special Deal, he

could not see himself overcoming his financial obstacles. Couden believed gray clouds always followed him. He didn't understand that his decisions, whether negative or positive, affected his life and dictated his direction.

With only 20 minutes to get to class, Couden rushed out the door and traveled to the other side of town. When he arrived to the Character Education Institute, there was a multitude of people from different ethnic backgrounds and age groups as well as social classes. He was very surprised to see so many people with character hardships just like him.

You see in Reality, Couden thought that only certain types of people had character issues. However, there are doctors, entertainers, athletes, business owners, lawyers, and many others who have experienced character challenges because of a poor reputation.

The class began and Couden started to drift away just as he did when he was in school. The instructor continued to lecture about reputation and how it affects character. The information was invaluable, but Couden ignored every word. He heard the instructor speaking but wasn't actively listening.

Every time the instructor spoke about a character pitfall, Couden wandered back in time when he made the same mistakes. Thinking back on how he managed to accumulate so many bad debts gave Couden a bad reputation. But what could he do? The debt was there, the collections were on his report and it seemed impossible to rebuild a negative reputation.

Couden was so consumed with his thoughts that he failed to realize the Character Education Institute was the right place to start over. Without proper education and knowledge of how character works, he could never begin to rebuild. He would be destined to make the same mistakes again.

A couple of hours went by and the class was wrapping up. Couden looked around the room at everyone's faces and saw that each person seemed to have a look of relief. He watched as everyone laughed and discussed with one another the key points they had learned in class. They joked about their situations now because they understood where the mistakes were made and how to correct them.

For the first time, Couden heard people use words like empowered, strengthened and sharpened when referring to how they felt after attending the class. Unfortunately, Couden was unable to think of a single word that described how he felt. Although the instructor had given solid advice and practical steps to developing better character, Couden missed the message. He was too busy wallowing in the past to open his mind to the future.

Before dismissing the class for a 15 minute break, the instructor announced that there would be a short exam.

"Exam, what exam?" Couden panicked since tests and exams were always his downfall in school.

One of the students noticed Couden was extremely nervous. He leaned over to offer some advice.

"Hey there, relax a little, this test will be easy!

"What if I get some of the answers wrong? I don't test very well," Couden whispered.

"If you listened to the lecture, the test should be a breeze. It's just a recap of the information taught during the class."

That was easy for him to say. Couden had barely heard a word the instructor said. When he had spoken to the representative a few months ago, she never said anything about completing an exam. If he had known that, he would have never agreed to attend the class. Determined to show the Special Deal Headquarters he was capable of taking the exam, he quickly glanced over some notes that one of the students left on their desk.

When the break was over the instructor asked everyone to take their seats and clear their desks. Couden tried to be confident but he was sure he was going to fail. He looked over the questions and tried to answer them as best he could, but he did not understand a single one. The quick review was no match for hours of instruction. Couden had to learn there is no quick fix for character improvement. The best way to move forward is to be educated on how to approach, handle and repair a negative reputation, so you can turn it into a positive one.

Angry and confused about what to do next, Couden finished the exam. He did the best he could do with the amount of information he retained, which wasn't much. Couden held his head down and walked out of the classroom depressed.

"I guess I'll go home and forget about changing my life. I probably failed the test and ruined my chances of getting the Special Deal again."

Couden sought refuge in his mother's basement. It made him feel secure and after the day he had, he needed a little attention for his mommy. Couden was almost relaxed when he heard his mother yell down the stairs for him to pick up the telephone. The Special Deal Headquarters was waiting to speak with him. Before he could even say hello the representative gave Couden more disappointing news.

"We are very disappointed to hear about your failure." At that moment, Couden realized he had definitely failed the exam.

"Although you were granted a second, as well as a third chance to receive the Special Deal, you still fell short of the requirements to receive it. The Special Deal Committee has decided that you cannot and will not qualify for the Special Deal unless you decide to change your life and develop the kind of reputation and character that deserves something special."

Couden was speechless. Instead of acknowledging his mistakes, he was appalled that the Special Deal Headquarters would call him at his mother's house and disrespect him in such a manner.

"First, how did you know I was here and second, how dare you tell me that I don't deserve something special!" Couden yelled at the representative.

Couden believed he had changed his life several

months ago when he tried to complete his requirements for the Special Deal. He was heated and ready to tell the representative just what to do with the Special Deal, when suddenly there was a loud click and the sound of a dial tone.

"I can't believe she just hung up the phone in the middle of our conversation and disregarded what I was about to say!"

Crazed with anger, Couden tried to call the Special Deal Headquarters to give them a piece of his mind. He was not going to let anyone talk to him that way and get away with it. Couden dialed the number to the Special Deal Headquarters, but instead of reaching a representative, he heard a recording saying the number was no longer valid and to check the number again.

"Can you believe this! What a scam! Someone called me less than five minutes ago from the Special Deal Headquarters and now the number is disconnected," Couden exclaimed. "Oh who cares anyway?

He's right. When you have nothing worth loosing, its impossible to care. Couden Careless had numerous chances to take advantage of the biggest opportunity in Reality, despite his character flaws and bad reputation. But instead of accepting his mistakes and learning how to improve his character so he could move forward, his flaws kept repeating, causing Couden to loose the one opportunity that could have changed his life. But in Reality, he couldn't care less about it one way or the other.

Any change, even a change for the better, is always accompanied by drawbacks and discomforts.
~ARNOLD BENNETT

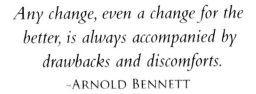

We can't keep doing the same things expecting different results

Chapter Ten

By Any Means

A child's appetite for new toys appeal to the desire for ownership and appropriation: the appeal of toys comes to lie not in their use but in their status as possessions.
~CHRISTOPHER LASCH

Dee Joneses leaned against the mailbox with her cell phone in hand. She figured it should be time for the Special Deal Headquarters to send her deal in the mail or at least give her a call to let her know when it would arrive. Either way, Dee was determined to get her Special Deal.

After all this time nothing had changed. She had the same mentality before the deal came...give me, give me, and give me more. She spent so much time waiting for the deal to arrive, she didn't eat or sleep and stopped caring about her appearance. Dee fell into depression and looked like a shell of her former flashy self.

Hours passed and there was no sign of the postmaster. Disappointed yet again, Dee pulled her weak, feeble body from the mailbox and staggered back into her home. Once inside, Dee slumped down on the sofa and watched a little television. She had to free her mind from the disappointment. Suddenly, a special message alert flashed across the television screen. It read:

This Is Your Last Chance!
Get This Great Deal Today!
Why wait for something special
when you can feel good right now.
Call now and have your character
card ready to BUY NOW!

Dee rubbed her eyes. At first she thought she was delirious, especially since she hadn't taken care of herself in a few weeks. But she wasn't delirious. Dee was overwhelmed with happiness and joy!

"You know that's right. Why wait for something special when I can feel good right now with something great?" Dee thought.

Eager to feel good for the moment, Dee grabbed the phone and called the number displayed on the screen. Before she knew it, she had bought her very own Great Deal. She figured this wouldn't hurt her chances of getting the Special Deal since it was a matter of time before she received it anyway. As an extra bonus for sacrificing food and much needed rest, Dee would have a Great Deal plus the Special Deal! Who could top that?

Dee imagined all the lavish things she could buy with both deals when there was a loud knock at the door. Dee managed to get up from the sofa and stagger to the front door. When she opened it she saw a certified letter on the porch.

"This was fast," Dee thought. "I wasn't expecting to receive the Great Deal so soon. I thought it would take at least 24 hours to arrive."

Dee slowly grabbed the letter. To her surprise the return address said Special Deal Headquarters. Beads of perspiration streamed down her forehead. Her hands started to shake nervously as she opened the envelope. The letter inside contained disturbing news and took Dee by surprise. It read:

Special Deal Headquarters

Dee Joneses
2 Keep Up Way
Reality, USA 24682

Ms. Joneses,

Thank you for your interest. Unfortunately, we are
unable to grant you the Special Deal at this time due to
your constant greed and unexceptional reputation which
has destroyed your character.

Several months ago we extended an offer asking you to
complete three simple requirements to help rebuild your
character. However, you fell short of fulfilling each one
properly, therefore ruining your chances of receiving
the Special Deal. Your desire to have more was far
greater then your desire to have freedom, not realizing
freedom will give you the opportunity to do more with
your life besides living beyond your means.

Your ability to acquire material possessions does not
compare to the ability to live out your dreams. As long
as you continue to view life this way, you will always
miss out on something special.

Good luck in the future.

Sincerely,
Special Deal Committee

Reading this letter caused Dee much heartache. Yet it was true. Dee Joneses allowed her greed and desire to have more than anyone else cloud her judgement. She could not see beyond the now, to wait for something that was truly special. Instead of maintaining a good reputation and positive character profile, Dee preferred keeping up with possessions that gave her the look of high society living.

Protect your reputation and use it to build good character. If not, you'll discover that keeping up with the Jones's, will keep you from experiencing the chance of a lifetime.

You can never get enough of what you don't need to make you happy.
~ERIC HOFFER

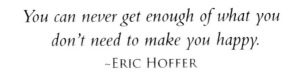

**We must remember that
our only competition is the
person we see each time
we look in the mirror**

Chapter Eleven

You Have To Do More

*We shall have no better conditions in
the future if we are satisfied with all
those which we have at present*
~THOMAS EDISON

Jestu Getby finally uncovered his fate regarding the
Special Deal. He found out about it at work. As he
walked down the hall to his desk, he started grumbling
out loud. He knew his coworkers could hear him.

"No one better bother me or say anything to me
today because I had a rough night and I don't want to
be entertained by someone else's drama," Jestu Getby
groaned.

Actually, everyone in the office ignored him. He
had almost arrived to his desk when he heard several

coworkers bragging about the Special Deal and how wonderful it was to receive something so great. Everyone was laughing and sharing stories about how the Special Deal was changing their lives. Jestu had forgotten about the Special Deal. Some time ago he had decided that he probably wouldn't be able to get the Special Deal. So he moved on with his life.

Once Jestu arrived to his desk, he quickly logged on his computer. He wanted to visit the Special Deal website and see what everyone was chattering about. There it was, the sign he had seen so many times before right on his screen. Those bold golden letters were hypnotic. The Special Deal is Coming! It's the Deal of a Lifetime, blah, blah, blah… As he read on, he saw stories from residents all over the city who had received the deal. He read how the deal had changed their lives. Some lives were changed forever.

One story Jestu read was from a single mother who had worked very hard to establish a better life for herself and her son. This single mother testified about how wonderful the deal was. She said that understanding character, making sacrifices to pay on time and balancing her spending had enabled her to secure the Special Deal. She concluded her story by expressing how she and her son will enjoy the benefits of the Special Deal for years to come.

Moved by the courageous story, Jestu started to think that maybe he had acted a little too hastily. Maybe he should not have abandoned the Special Deal several months earlier. He continued to navigate through the testimonials when he came to another story that interested him. This story was about a young man who learned early on that there is a thin line between character use and reputation abuse.

The young man had destroyed his reputation and did not known how to fix it. Then he heard about the Special Deal and empowered himself to learn about establishing good character and a strong reputation. As a result of the hard work put into correcting the young man's character deficiencies, he was now on the right track to character recovery and was able to secure the Special Deal.

"These people were all just lucky," Jestu thought.

He believed the stories were too good to be true, until he stumbled upon a story that was from a coworker who sat right beside him. As Jestu read her story he was amazed to see how she overcame her situation. It was just like his.

The coworker wasn't educated about having good character or a solid reputation. She thought it was too hard to stay on track when you didn't make much money. She had to realize that it is not how much money you make but how much money you spend that affects your reputation and determines your character.

As Jestu continued to read her story, he learned that after she secured her Special Deal, she used it to make much needed improvements in her life. But, before she could receive the deal, she had to educate herself and fulfill the requirements to improve her conditions. Now she was embarking on a new path that allowed her to leave her present job and secure a more fulfilling career all because she had received the Special Deal.

Jestu finished her story with mixed emotions. He was a little jealous because someone he knew was actually leaving the dead-end establishment he had called work for the past several years. He was also disappointed because he realized that he could have had similar things happen to him. If only he had taken the initiative and the time to do those extra requirements to secure his Special Deal.

Just when the situation could not get any worse, Jestu received an email from the Special Deal Headquarters. He had hoped that maybe today would be his lucky day. That there was still a chance for him to receive the Special Deal. Reluctantly he opened the email and braced himself for whatever the message said. It read:

To: Jestu_Getby@mediocre.com
From: Special_Deal_Committee@SDH.com
Subject: Special Deal Status
SDHeadquarters

Thank you for interest in the Special Deal.
However due to your lack of drive and
unwillingness to improve your current situation,
we are unable to grant you the Special Deal.

Furthermore, we don't have anything else to say
to you because we don't feel like putting forth the
effort to write more about your situation.

Good luck in the future.

Sincerely,
Special Deal Committee

Jestu could not believe what he was reading. He felt slighted by the Special Deal Headquarters. He was hoping to have another chance, but in Reality you only get so many chances to change.

The message was true. Jestu Getby missed opportunities to progress because of his poor reputation and character. You cannot spend your life just trying to get by, or you will close the door to opportunities that lead to freedom.

Don't let your special character and values,
the secret that you and no one else does,
the truth—don't let that get swallowed
up by the great chewing complacency.
~AESOP

**We must avoid having a false
sense of security and realize
in order to have more we
must do more and be more.**

The Day After

Back to Reality

*Reality is merely an illusion, albeit
a very persistent one.*
~ALBERT EINSTEIN

Tugood Tubetru, Dee Joneses, Jestu Getby and Couden Careless all learned their fate regarding the Special Deal. Some did not accept the outcome; nevertheless the decisions were made.

Of the four characters depicted in our story, Tugood Tubetru was the resident who received the Special Deal. He was the one who understood the benefits of having a solid reputation which ultimately affects character. He knew how to make his reputation work for him-not against him. Some may think that Tugood Tubetru is just that-too good to be true. However, in our reality, there are dozens of residents just like him who receive "special deals" everyday, but not without hard work.

Tugood Tubetru, Dee Joneses, Jestu Getby and Couden Careless live in all of us to some degree. It's up to you to determine which characteristic will dominate.

Do you want to live your life dodging responsibility? Do you want to always breath a sigh of relief at the end of each month because you just made it? Do you feel as though you have to spend all your earnings to portray a lifestyle that is nothing more than a facade?

Do you want to be in control of your future and prepared for emergencies? Do you want to be confident if potential employers check your reputation and character background? Can you depend on your reputation and character like a friend when you need to?

How you answer these questions will determine your ability to handle something special.

So in reality, what Special Deal
are you waiting for?

THE END

"Hard work spotlights the character of people: some turn up their sleeves, some turn up their noses, and some don't turn up at all."
~RALPH RANSOM

Financial Success Plan

*6 Steps to Creating Your
Financial Success Plan*

*How to Gain & Maintain Control
of your Personal Finances*

*Our goals can only be reached through a
vehicle of a plan, in which we must fervently
believe, and upon which we must vigorously
act. There is no other route to success.*
~PABLO PICASSO

E stimating income and expenditures for a set period of time is the foundation of the Financial Success Planning process. Unfortunately most of us don't take the time to create a plan or if we do create it, we lack the discipline to follow it. Creating a Financial Success Plan will allow you to indicate your ability to save and invest, analyze your standard of living, determine if you're living within or beyond your means, highlight any problem areas and identify holes or gaps in your financial life.

While it can be overwhelming to sit down and go through all of your expenses and set limits for your spending, it's a great way to change your financial future for the better. If you don't know how much money you have coming in and going out, it will be much harder to get ahead and achieve your financial goals.

6 Benefits to having a Financial Success Plan

Provides Control
A Financial Success Plan is the key to enable you to take charge of your finances. With a Financial Success Plan, you have the tools to decide exactly what's going to happen to your hard earned money, where each dollar goes and when it leaves.

Increases Communication
A Financial Success Plan is a communication tool that creates a structured opportunity to talk with family members or other invested parties to discuss the priorities for where your money is being spent and where it should be spent. Communication eliminates the guess work and insecurities that come with not knowing what's going on.

Identify Opportunities

Knowing the exact state of your personal monetary affairs, and being in control of them, allows you to take advantage of opportunities that you might otherwise miss. The key is to develop seven streams of income that will help you build financial security.

Extra Money

A budget may produce extra money for you to use it as you wish. Hidden fees and lost interest paid to outsiders may be eliminated. Unnecessary expenditures, once identified, can be eliminated. Savings, even small ones, can be invested and made to work for you.

Money Management

You can make better use of your income and maintain better control of your expenditures if you have a clear idea of what you own and what you owe.

Saving

Remember to treat yourself like a bill and write the first check out monthly to You Inc.

Knowing precisely how much is left over after deducting the current liabilities provides a strong incentive to save. As you see your net worth increase, you will be encouraged to help it grow.

Now that you know the benefits, it's time to create your own plan for financial success. With anything you do in life a plan is crucial. Without a plan you may find yourself lost, stumbling throughout life by default. After your plan has been created, go full steam ahead to your desired destiny and enjoy the life you were designed to live.

6 Steps to Create a Sound Financial Plan

Step 1 Identify Goals and Objectives
Step 2 Gather Data
Step 3 Analyze & Evaluate Your Financial Status
Step 4 Develop a Plan
Step 5 Implement the Plan
Step 6 Monitor the Plan & Make Necessary Adjustments

Step 1-Identify Goals and Objectives

Identify both financial and personal goals and objectives as well as clarify your financial and personal values and attitudes. These may include providing for children's education, supporting elderly parents or relieving immediate financial pressures which would help maintain your current lifestyle and provide for retirement.

Examples
- To create a strategy to save and use your gifts and talents to build additional income.
- To identify your personal strengths and weaknesses as it relates to your personal finances. To provide a strategy to further your financial success and stability.
- To develop guidelines for the earning, saving and spending financial resources.

Step 2-Gather Data

Clarify your present situation by collecting and assessing all relevant financial data. Once you're able to see what's pending, what you're paying and what you have, you will have a good snapshot of where you stand financially.

Examples
- Create a list of your assets and liabilities.
- Gather your tax returns, records of securities transactions, insurance policies, wills, pension plan and all other important documents.
- Compile all outstanding bills and notices and record who they're from and the amounts owed.
- List your additional available resources.

Step 3-Analyze & Evaluate Your Financial Status

This will allow you to address or uncover financial problems that create barriers to achieve financial independence. These possible problem areas must be identified before solutions can be found.

Examples

- To little or too much insurance coverage.
- A potential high tax burden.
- Your cash flow may be inadequate.
- Current investments may not be winning the battle with changing economic times.

Step 4-Develop a Plan

Controlling your financial affairs requires a plan. You must budget and track your expenses to have a strong sense of where your money goes in order to reach your financial goals.

Examples

- Saving for a down payment on a house.
- Starting a college or university fund for your children.
- Buying a new car.
- Paying off the credit cards.
- Planning for retirement.

Step 5-Implement the plan

It's not enough to just create the plan; we must also use the plan.

Examples
- The key is to start with small steps.
- Become accustomed to the steps in order to repeat them consistently.

Step 6-Monitor and Review

The Financial Success Plan must be reviewed and revised periodically to ensure that it's working effectively to achieve your goals and has the most recent data.

Examples
- Re-asses your plan at least once a year to account for changes in your life, finances and debt and current economic conditions.
- Create new goals to add to your plan as your needs change.

As you complete your plans for financial success, remember the **5 Knows:**
- Know where you are financially
- Know exactly how much money you have to work with
- Know how your funds are allocated
- Know how your funds are working for you
- Know how far along you are toward reaching your goals

Quick notes

- Always pay when due, even if it's the minimum. Pay when due is the magic phrase that will help protect your credit.
- Create a Financial Success Plan and use it as a road map to guide you where you want to be.
- Don't live outside of your means.
- Keep important documents on file; anything that can later verify proof of payments or closed accounts. The burden of proof is on you.
- Communicate with creditors.
- Make payment arrangements where possible and when needed. Creditors/utilities just want their money and they appreciate you being proactive and taking responsibility. Often they will work with you.
- Always pay late fees. These can accumulate and cause your accounts to become past due and possibly fall into collections.
- Keep balances of credit cards below 30% of the limit if possible.
- Always be open to creating multiple streams of income that make sense.
- Review the terms of all accounts. Read the small print.
- Beware of high interest rates on payday loans (any loan for that matter).
- Don't close old credit accounts.

You can find **Clyde Anderson** every Saturday on the CNN Weekend Newsroom where *Clyde* has served as a CNN contributing finance expert since 2006. *Clyde* also serves as a nationally acclaimed speaker, commentator, consultant, author, and trainer covering topics from the state of the housing market to maximizing a budget in a changing economy. *Clyde* has a rich history in the housing and finance sector that spans more than a decade. Giving back to his community is the cornerstone of *Clyde's* success. In addition to his financial endeavors, *Clyde* is a also a successful entrepreneur and believes small business is the cornerstone of America. *Clyde* holds a BA in Business Management from Clark Atlanta University and resides with his family in Atlanta. He is available for keynote opportunities, panel discussions and media inquires.

For More Information Visit:

www.clydeandersononline.com

CPSIA information can be obtained at www.ICGtesting.com
Printed in the USA
LVOW10s0334130416

483252LV00012B/77/P